STARFISH
COLORING BOOK

Get FREE printable coloring pages and discounted book prices sent straight to your e-mail inbox every week!

Sign up at:
www.adultcoloringworld.net

Copyright © 2017 Adult Coloring World
All rights reserved.
ISBN-13: 978-1542367936
ISBN-10: 154236793X

PREVIEWS:

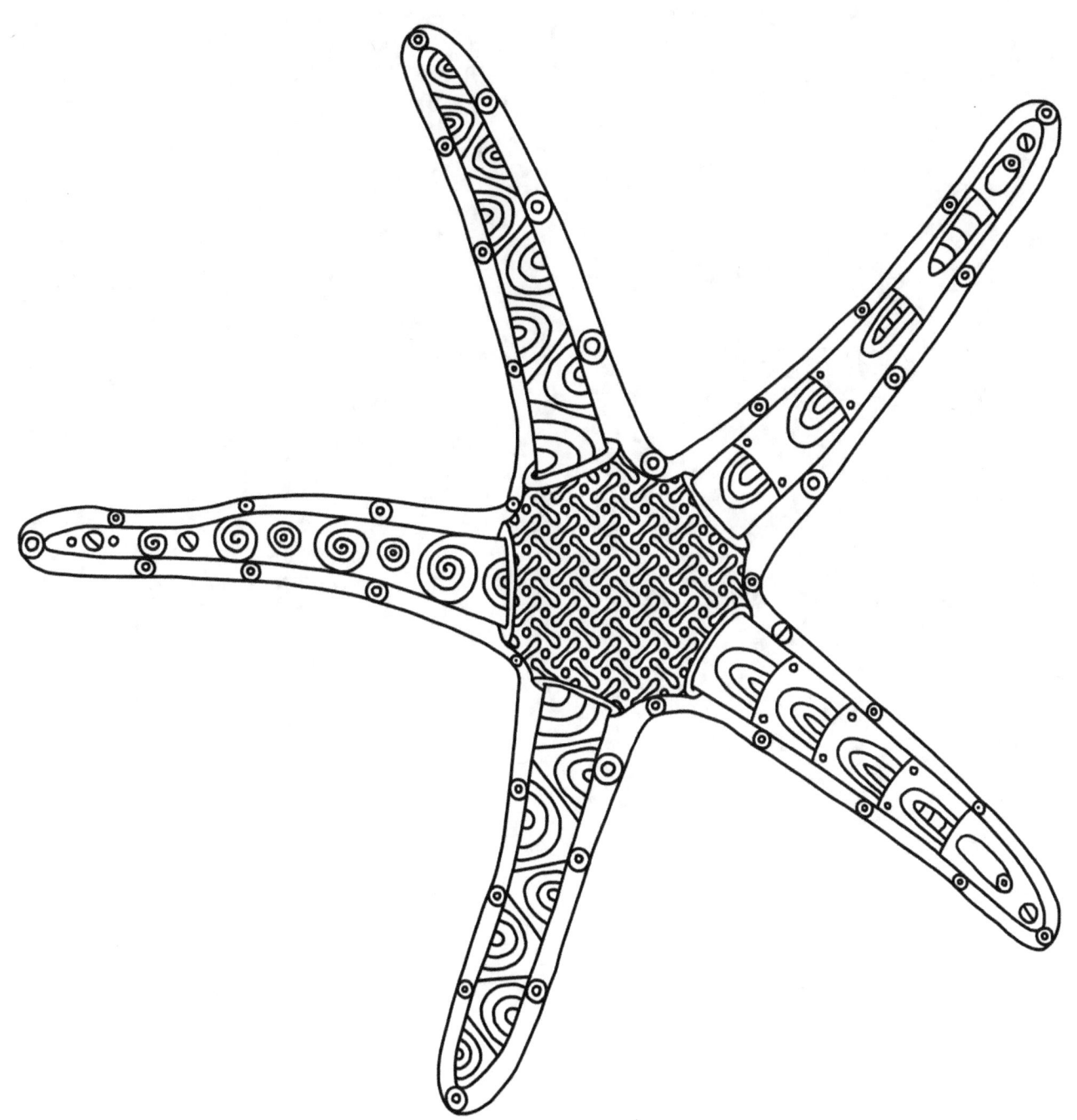

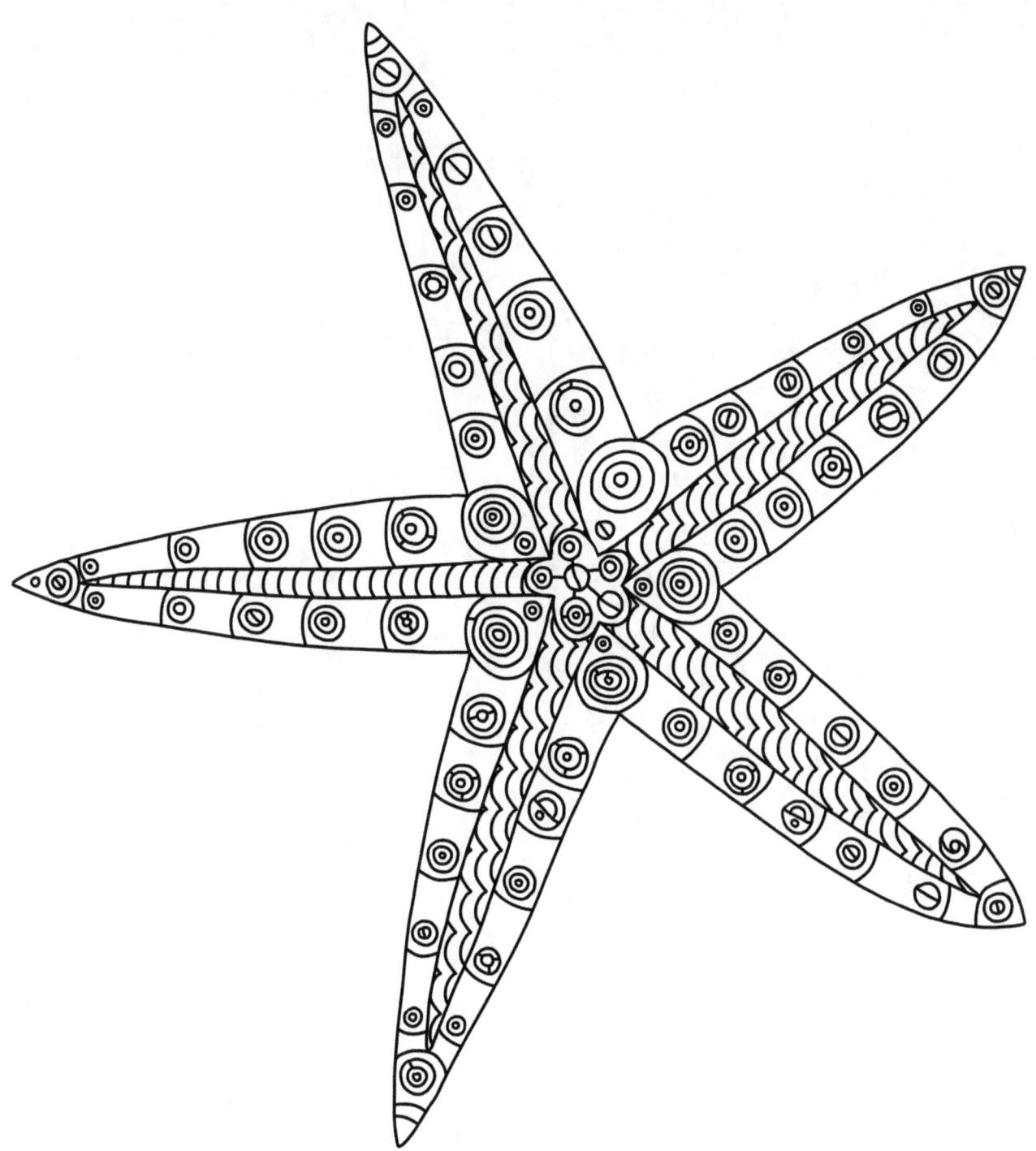

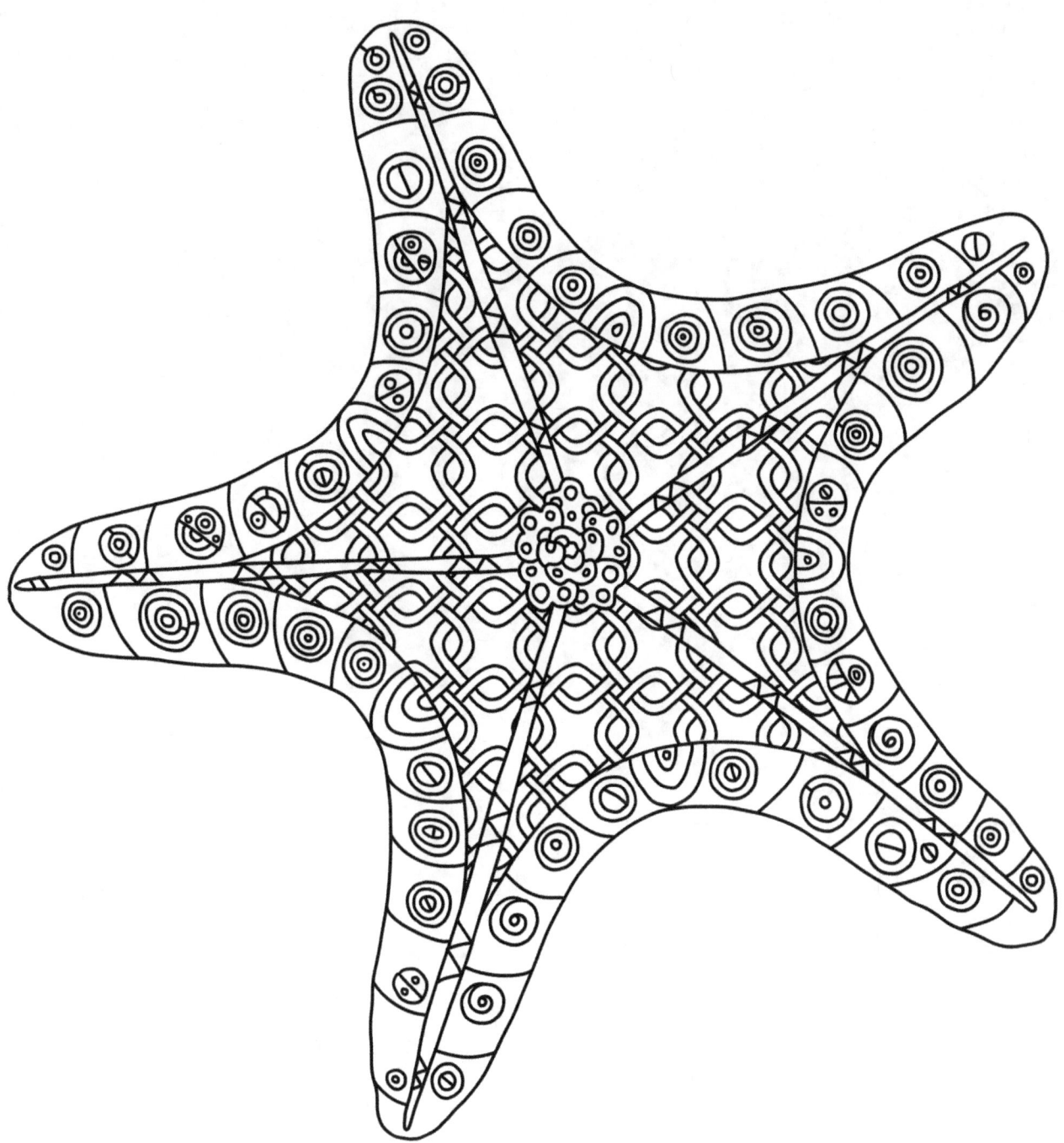

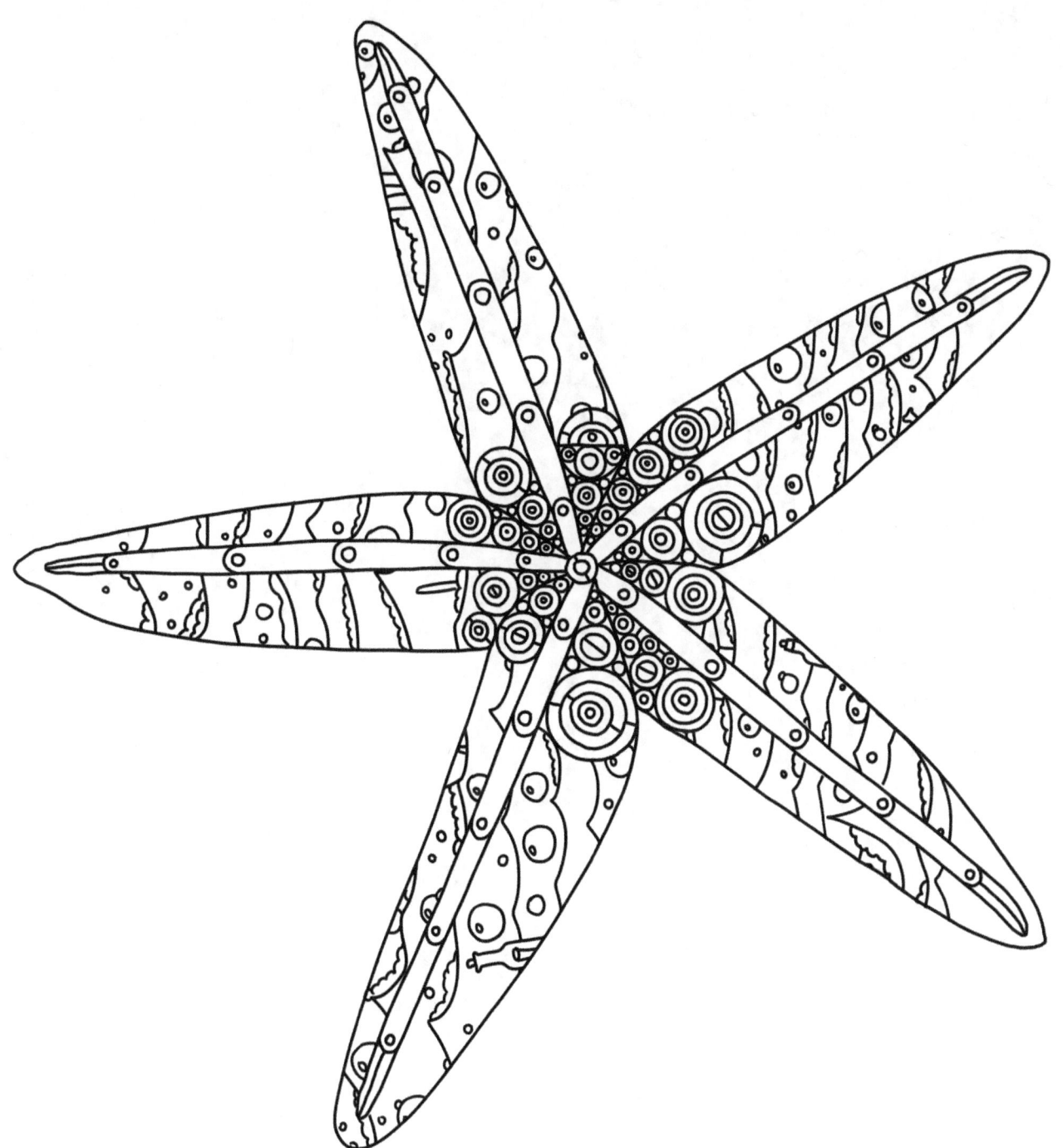

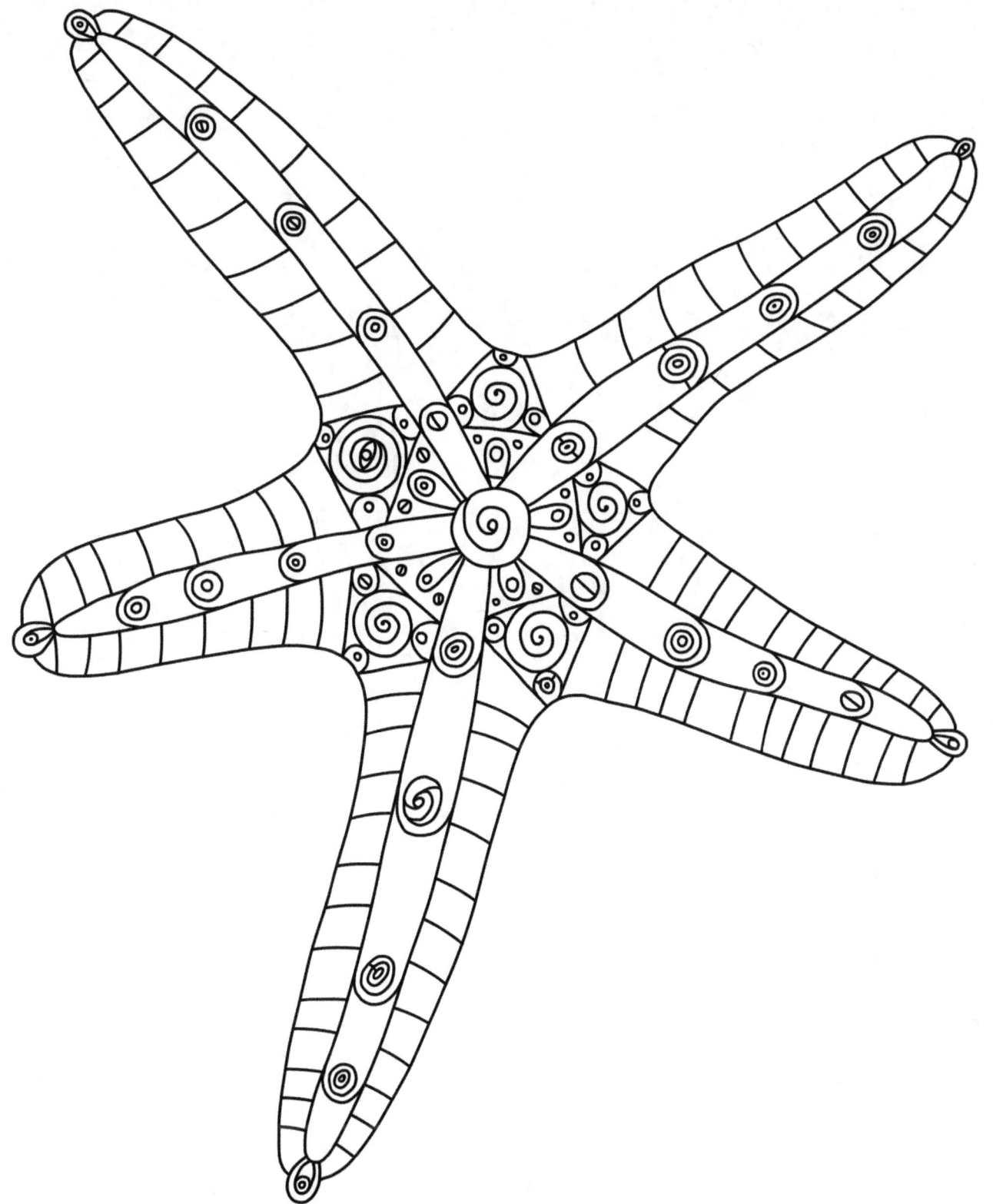

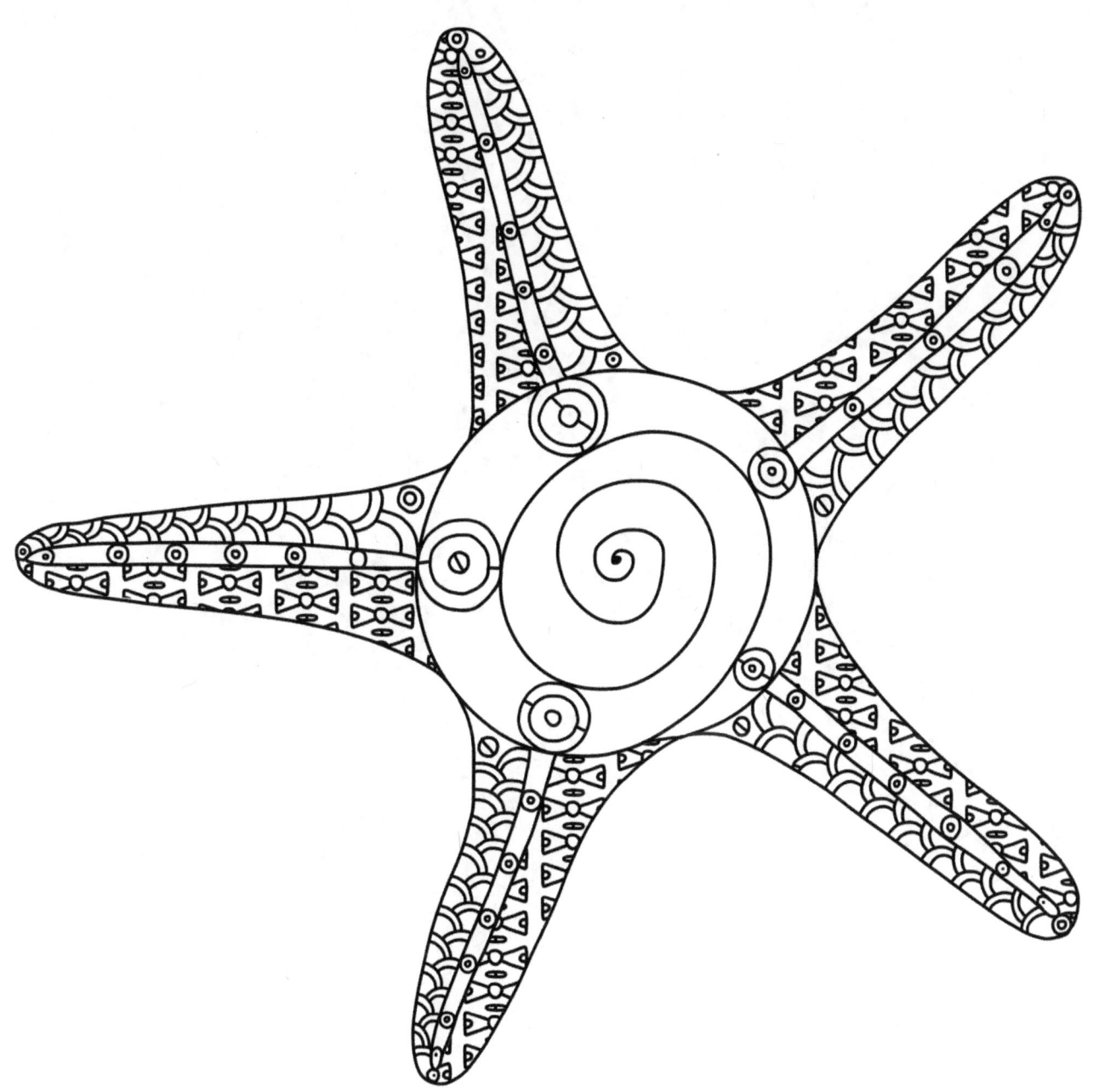

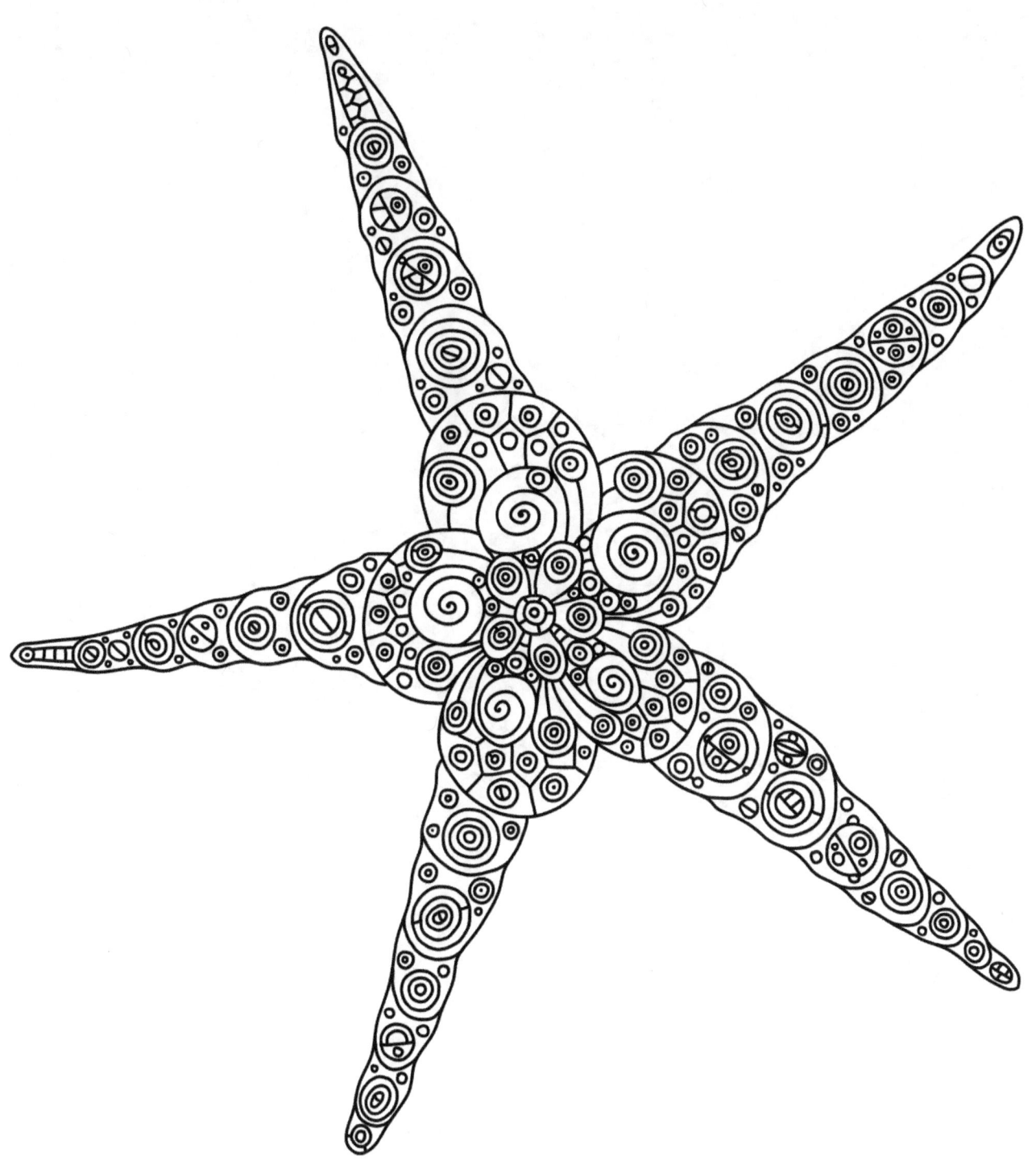

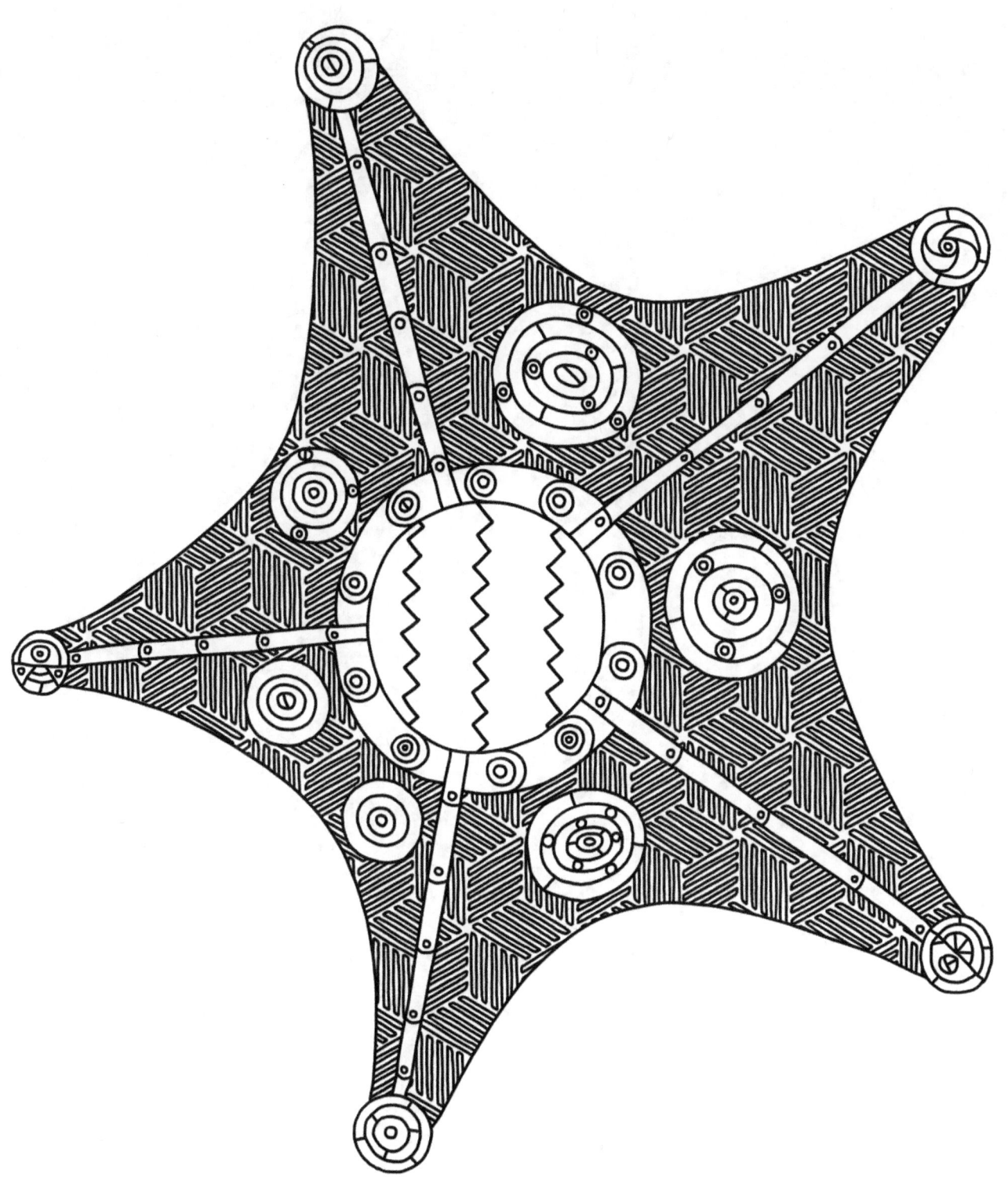

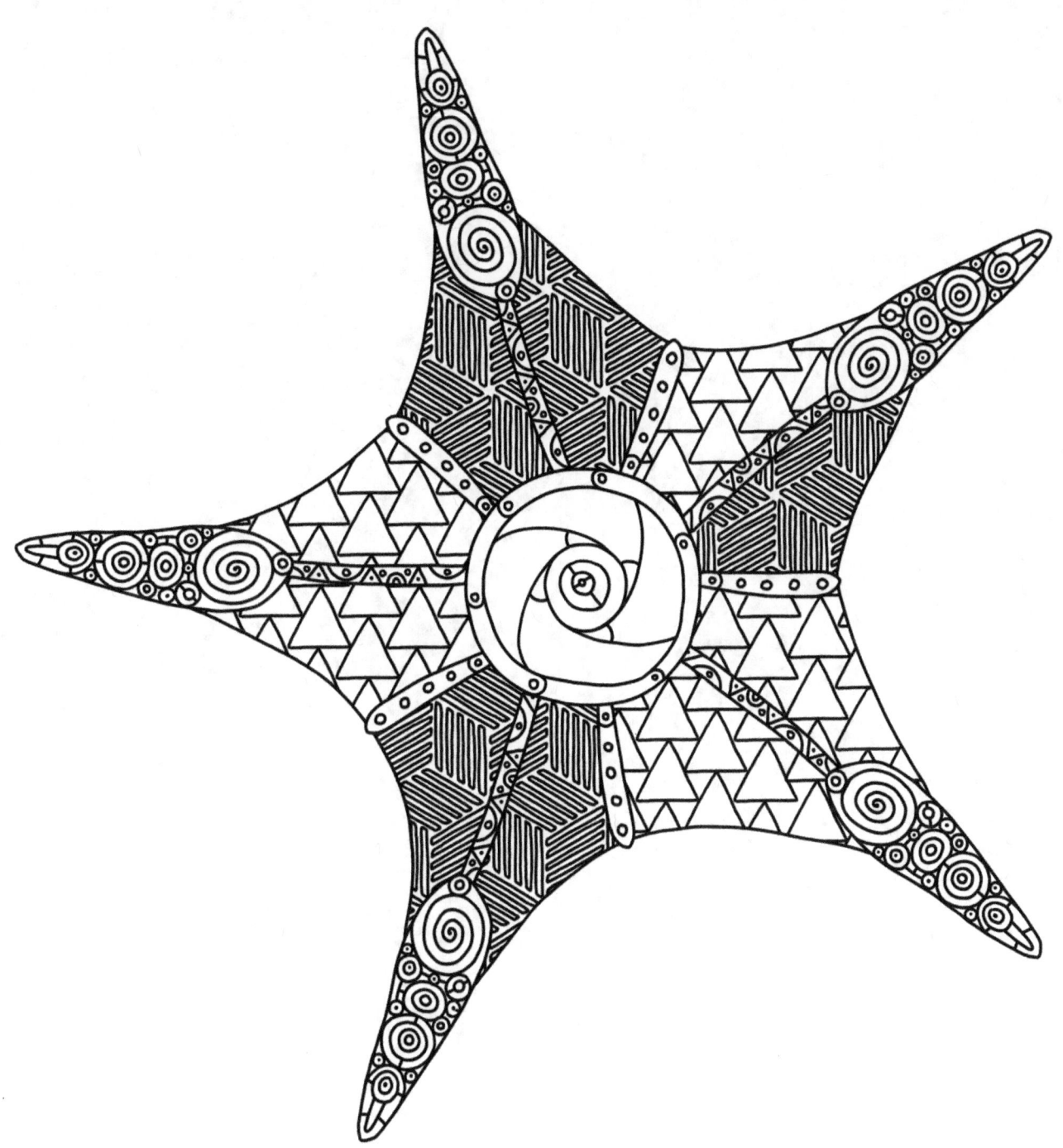

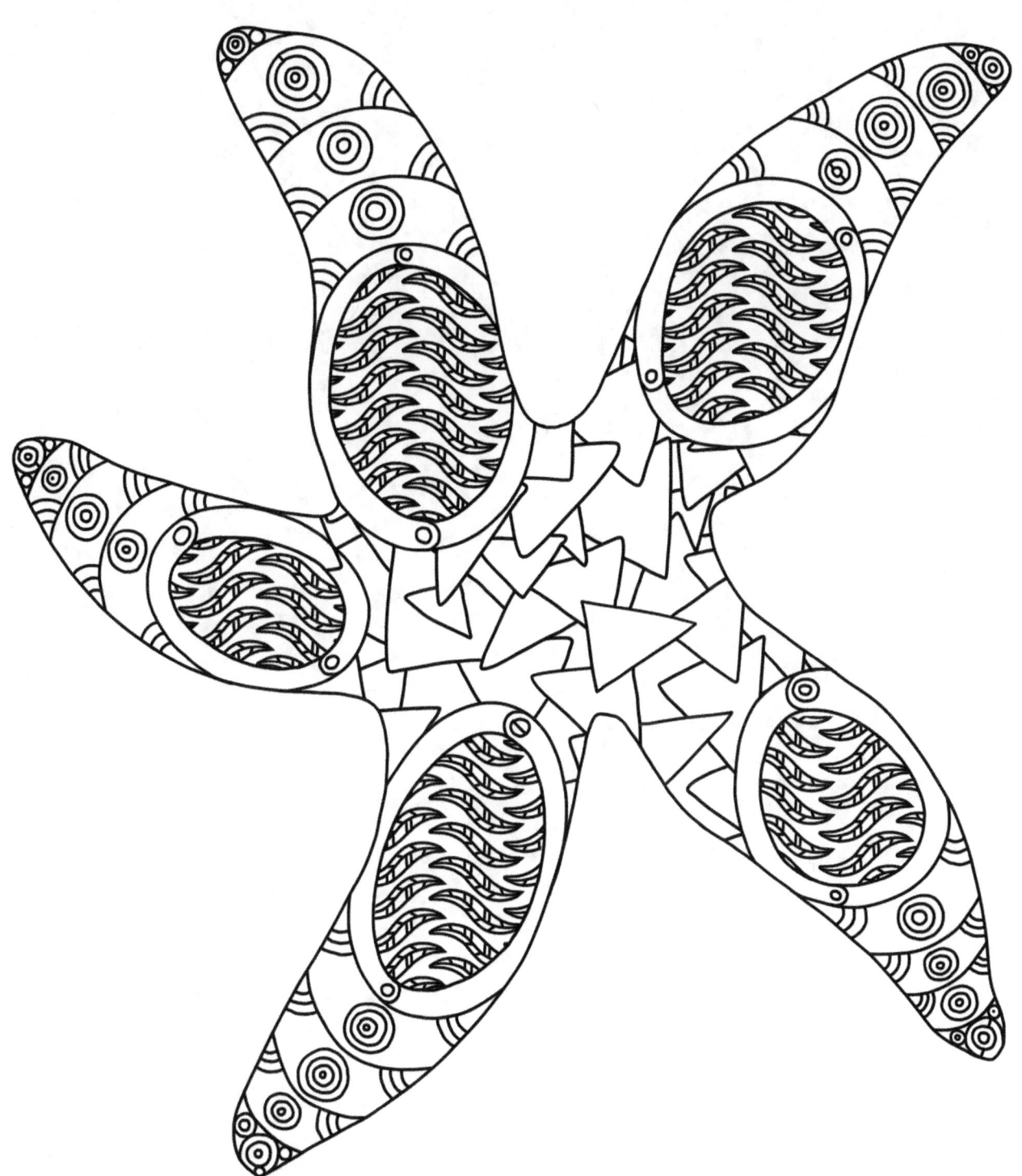

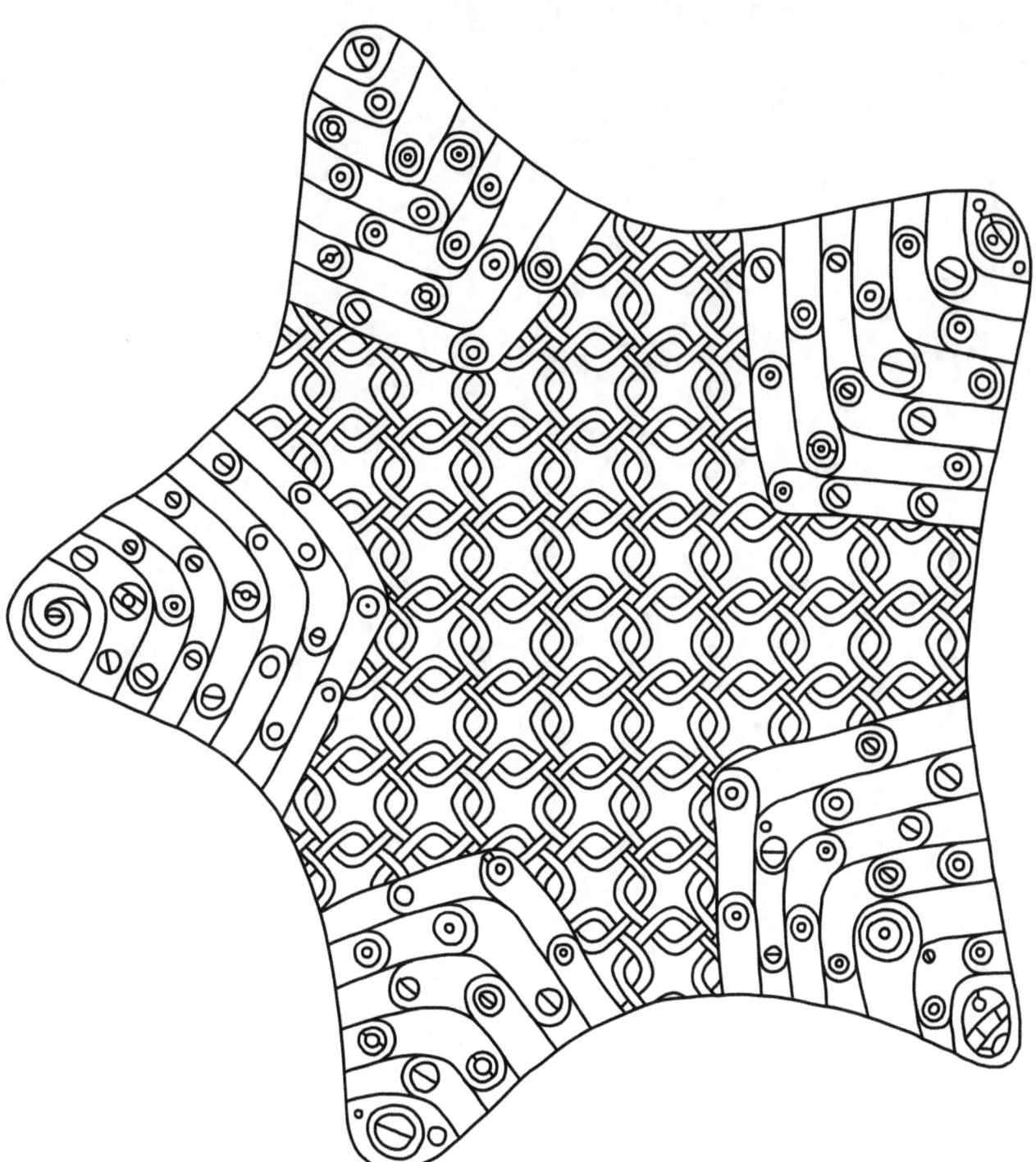

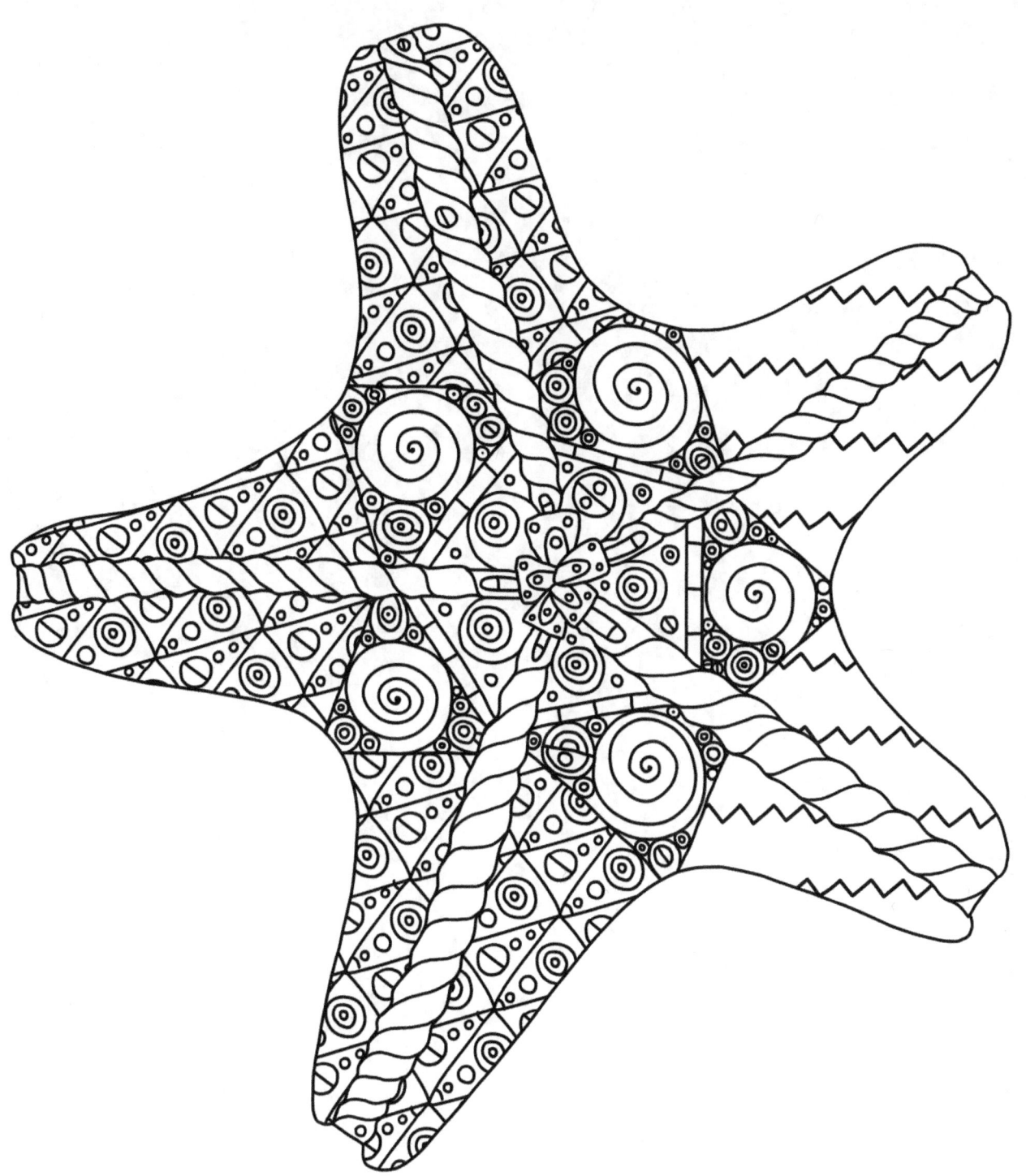

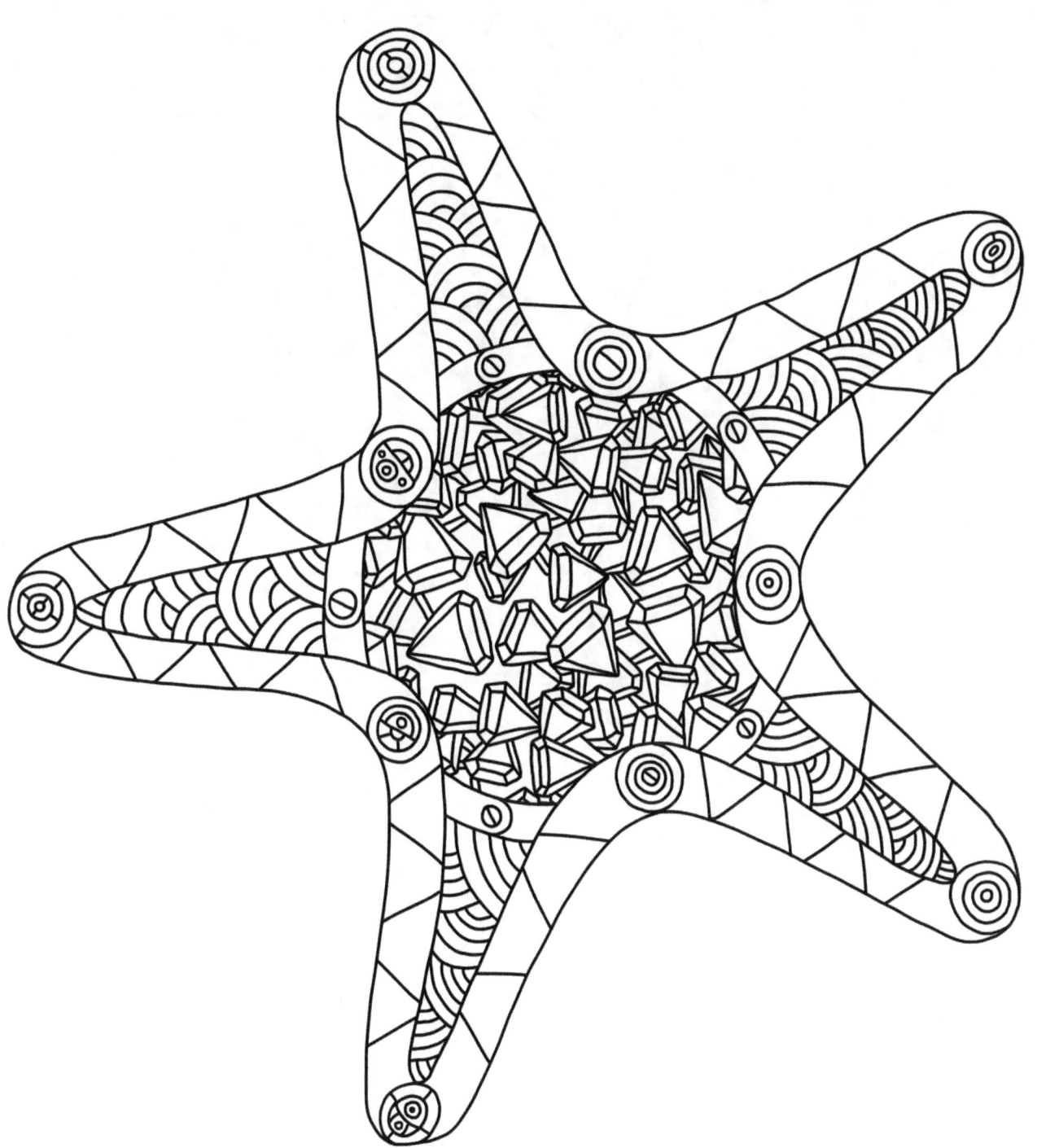

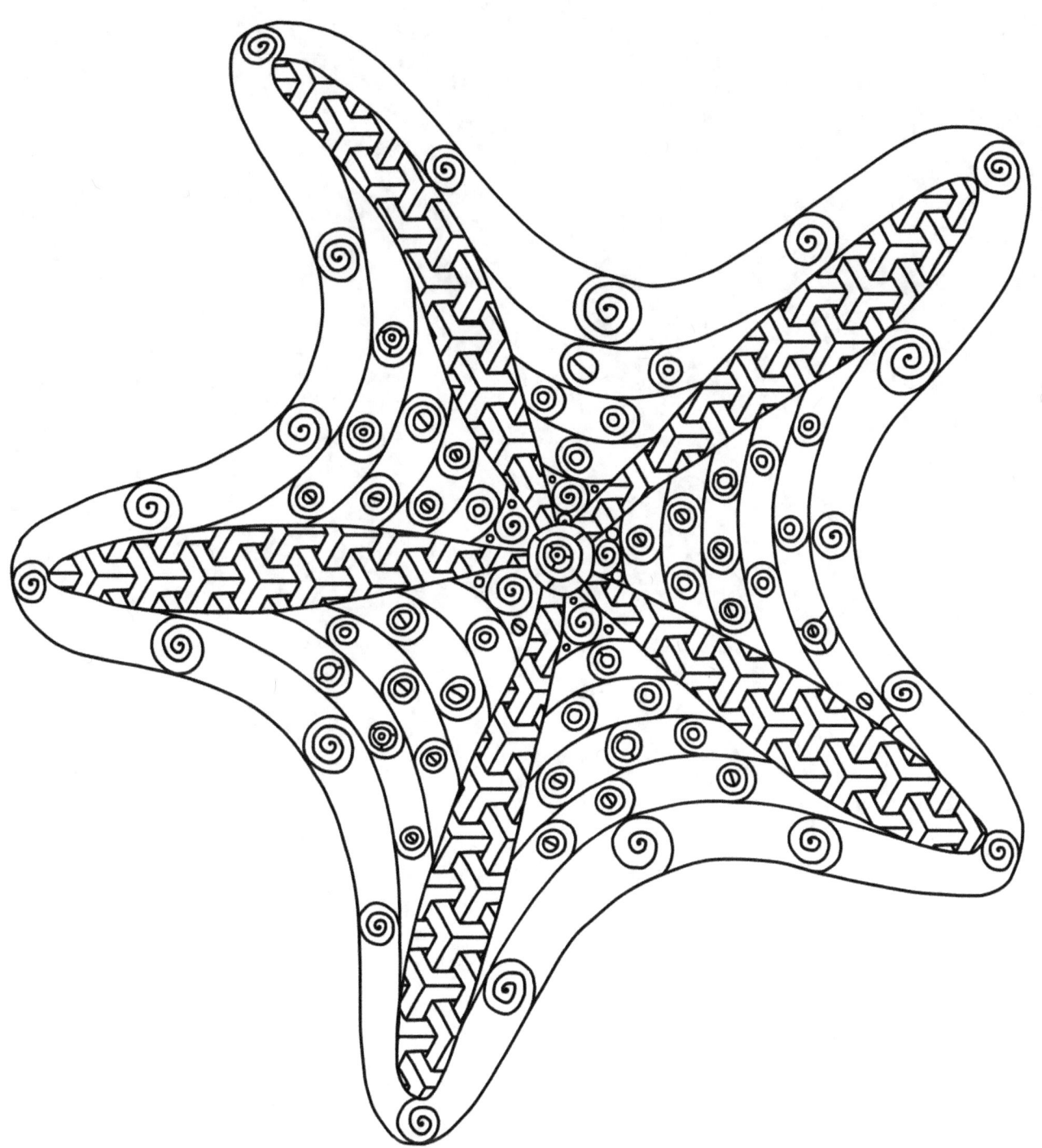

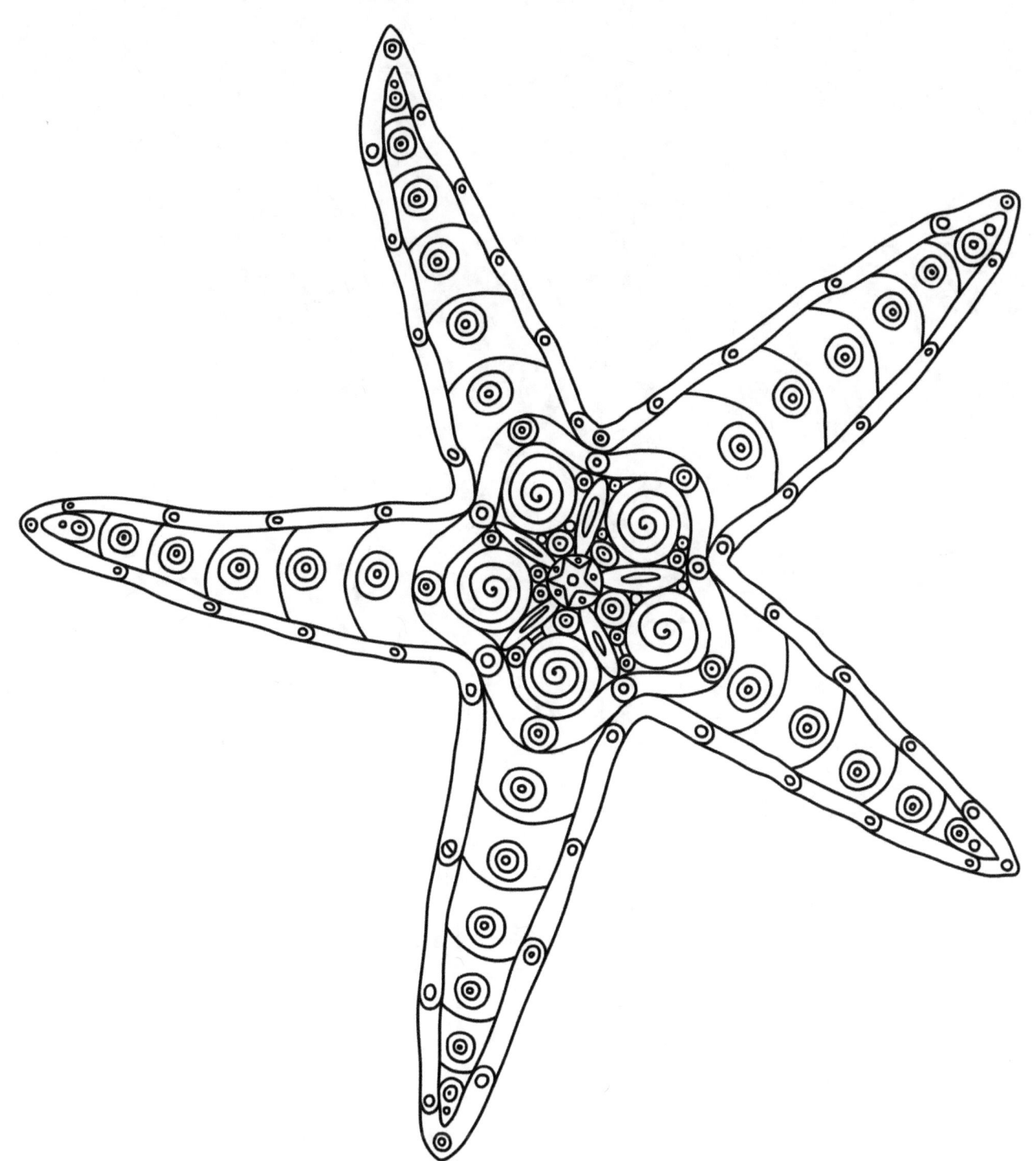

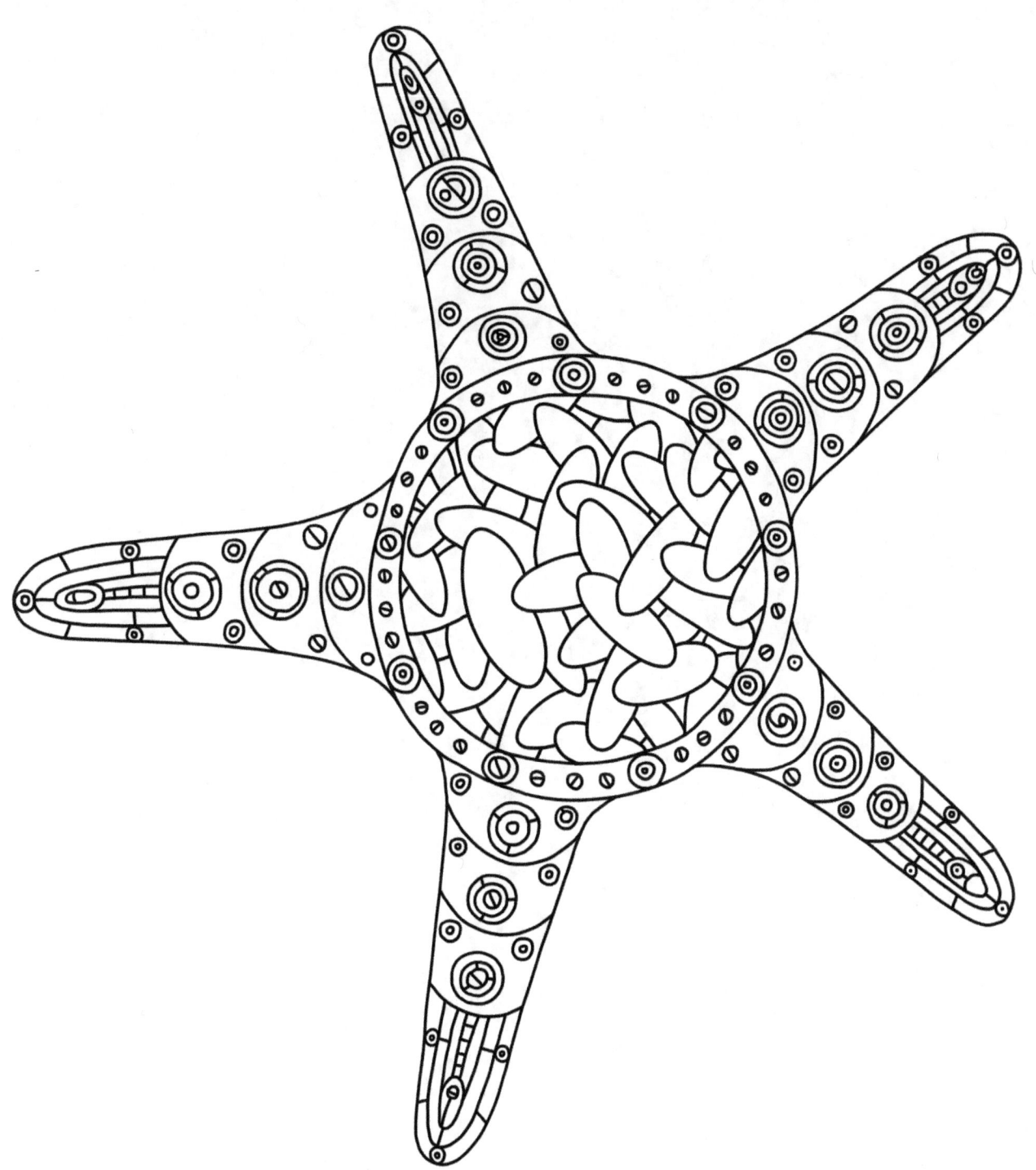

COLOR TEST PAGE

COLOR TEST PAGE

www.ingramcontent.com/pod-product-compliance
Lightning Source LLC
Chambersburg PA
CBHW051948280526
45789CB00009B/3209